TEN THINGS I LIKE ABOUT AFRICA'S RICHEST MAN

By

DON BERNADATE

Copyright reserved. No part of this book may be reproduced without the written consent of the author.

DEDICATION

TO ALL WHO WANT TO LEARN FROM OTHERS

GREAT LEADERS LESSONS SERIES

Are books written with the following in mind:

1. To enable readers learn great lessons from the lives of great men and achievers.

2. To see qualities that they should emulate.

3. To learn vital business steps from others.

4. To pick up a few tips on how to succeed in life.

RULES FOR WRITING THE GREAT LEADERS LESSONS SERIES

1. Writers must be brief.

2. Writers must call a spade a spade.

3. The great leader under reference must be a public

figure and achiever in his area of focus.

4. The book must be based on verifiable facts.

LESSON ONE

HE DID NOT ALLOW HIS LOWLY BIRTH TO STOP HIM.

Born in northern Nigeria, to a family that need to work twelve hours a day to feed, AL haji Dangote cannot be said to be born with a silver spoon. He needed to go out and earn a living like any other person but in his case, there were limitations because of the environment at the time when everyone willing to work just had to work for the government. His parents were not rich enough to raise him a loan. He had to go to an uncle who loaned him the start-up trading capital.

LESSON TWO

HE DID NOT ALLOW PRIDE TO STOP HIM.

He went to the uncle and asked for the loan. Many of us pride keep us down all our lives. We are too proud to be let down. We are too proud to fail. We do not want people to mock us but who cares if you succeed in the end.

There are many people out there who need help but foolish pride keeps them back from going to ask for help from those who would have gladly helped them.

LESSON THREE

HE IS A MAN WITH AN EYE OUT FOR OPPORTUNITIES.

He kept his eyes peeled for money making opportunities and when they came, he grabbed them and invested in them. He looked out for the basic needs of man, the very things that people make use of every day and things that man can hardly do without and he set out to exploit those needs.

He knew that the only way to make money is to solve people's problems and he set out to do just that and of course, he smiled to the bank.

LESSON FOUR

HE MADE HIS CHOICE AND FOCUSED ON IT.

Most of his mates at the time were busy partying but this young man refrained. There were vices that he could have picked up but he did not. He kept his cool and kept focused on where he was going, resisting all manners of peer pressure.

LESSON FIVE

HE HUMBLED HIMSELF AND LEARNT THE ROPES OF TRADING.

It has been said that if you do not learn how to drive, either you hit somebody or somebody would hit you. To start anything without first learning, is the fastest way to disaster. Today, there are many youths that want to build castles in the air and dream of owning islands in Eldorado but are not willing to learn a trade that would be a plank to the place they hope to be.

Though the richest man in Africa had been to the university, he did not mind going back to be an apprentice. He learned the ropes from his uncle. It was at a time when being to the university meant that you could get a "big man' job from the government but the young man was willing to learn and understand what he was stepping into.

LESSON SIX

HE HAS BEEN VERY CONSISTENT.

For over thirty years now, he has been in business and remained in business. Considering the fact that he is from Africa where rich business men easily buy themselves into political power, one would have thought that this man would make a foray into politics. But he has not. When military coups were popular, business men sponsored soldiers to overthrow legitimate governments but the name of this man has never been associated with any such infractions.

Even in these days of mushrooming democracy in Africa, the man has consistently resisted the temptation to join partisan politics. Instead, he has remained neutral and a friend of the government of the day- a much needed move to protect his investments.

LESSON SEVEN

HE GIVES BACK TO THE SOCIETY.

This man has shown that he is not a pirate with the self-serving philosophy of winner takes all. As his business is thriving, he has made it a duty to give back to the society. His companies are known for their corporate social responsibility. He has a number of times, come out in aid of victims of both man-made and natural disasters.

He is currently collaborating with Bill Gates and others in reducing some diseases in Nigeria.

LESSON EIGHT

HE REWARDS HIS WORKERS WELL.

This is to be seen in the fact that his workers, numbering into millions, have never been known to be on strike for any reason. Another pointer to this fact is that whenever he advertises for the position of lorry drivers, one of the least paid positions in his chain of companies, even PhD holders apply. They say where the carcass is, there the eagles gather. Surely, if you put sugar on the table, the ants will come.

Our subject is said to have exemplary incentives that have enabled him to attract the top cream of professionals and as you know, a company is as good as the company it keeps.

LESSON NINE

HIS BUSINESSES ARE DIVERSIFIED.

Al haji Dangote has not put all his eggs in one basket. He has interests in both quoted and non-quoted companies. He also trades on almost everything you can imagine. As we speak, he is building a refinery in Lagos as well as trading in cement and allied products.

LESSON TEN

HE IS A RISK TAKER.

Of course, you would rightly point out that every business man is a risk taker. Much as you may not be wrong, the fact remains that risk has levels. Some people would not venture beyond their state of residence. Al haji Dangote is a business man sans frontiers! He is not intimidated by such evils as terrorism, xenophobia, indigenization and other things that keep mere mortals home. He has his businesses spread out across several nations.

He is not just a risk taker, he is bold and courageous and heaven favors the audacious.

www.ingramcontent.com/pod-product-compliance
Lightning Source LLC
Chambersburg PA
CBHW031525210526
45464CB00007B/3027